MOON MAGICK OF THE TRIPLE GODDESS

Wiccan Moon Rituals, Lunar Spells, and Drawing Down the Moon

By Didi Clarke

Disclaimer:
While I have performed all these spells myself, your results may vary.

*If you'd like to be notified when I publish a new book or have something exciting in the works, be sure to sign up for my mailing list. You'll receive a **FREE** color magick correspondence chart when you do! Follow this link to subscribe:*

https://mailchi.mp/01863952b9ff/didi-clarke-mailing-list

CONTENTS

Chapter 1: The Magick of the Moon..2

Chapter 2: The Moon Phases...5

Chapter 3: Understanding the Triple Goddess 9

Chapter 4: New Moon Banishing Spell 12

Chapter 5: Full Moon Blessing Spell 17

Chapter 6: Waxing Moon Spell for a Fresh Start 21

Chapter 7: Waning Moon Dream Spell 25

Chapter 8: Selene Invocation 30

Chapter 9: Hecate Invocation 35

Chapter 10: Esbat Celebration 40

Chapter 11: Blue Moon Ritual 45

Chapter 12: Drawing Down the Moon 48

Chapter 13: Embrace the Divine Moon 54

Chapter 14: Read More From Didi Clarke...55

By Didi Clarke

CHAPTER 1: THE MAGICK OF THE MOON

Wiccans and witches are freethinkers. Our beliefs are guided by personal intuition and insight, which means that they're often wildly different from one person to another. This diversity of ideas is what makes the world of witchcraft the interesting place that it is—but there is one thing that unites almost all of us. And that thing is the moon.

The moon in Wicca is similar in importance to the cross in Christianity. It is one of the most central symbols of our faith and a source of spiritual power and inspiration that guides our magickal lives. It represents Divine power and is Divine power. It can bless and banish. It can reveal the wisdom of the spirit world to us.

To a witch, the moon is all this and much more. It may be our familiar celestial friend, but it always has new mysteries to reveal to us. It is a subject that we spend our lives growing to love but is also a subject we will never fully master.

However, through study and practice, we can learn to harness the power of the moon and use it to bring our will to life through the art of magick. The moon is always in flux, and by charting its monthly journey, we can align ourselves with its shifting energies.

What You'll Find In This Book

Within the pages of *Moon Magick of the Triple Goddess*, you'll find everything you need to get started harnessing the power of the moon in your own spellwork.

To begin with, we'll take a look at the phases of the moon and what they represent within Wicca. As the moon moves from one phase to another, its spiritual energies shift as well. This means that certain types of magick will be more effective at certain points in the month more than others. I'll show you the ins and outs of this monthly process and how to plan your spells and rituals for maximum potency.

Next, we'll get to know the Triple Goddess. This deity is one of the principal figures within Wicca and is associated closely with the moon. Learning the different aspects of the Triple Goddess and how they align with the phases of the moon is absolutely essential for this type of magick you're going to be performing. She is our celestial mother and a recurrent figure within moon magick, which is why I've dedicated an entire chapter to her.

Next up are the rituals themselves. Some of these spells correspond to different phases of the moon, while others have to do with unique lunar events (like a blue moon). These spells include magick for:

- Banishment
- Blessing
- A Fresh Start
- Dream Interpretation
- Much More!

I've also included a couple invocations to Goddesses associated with the moon—in addition to the Triple Goddess, there are a number of other powerful moon deities that you can call upon.

Finally, the book closes with a ritual for Drawing down the Moon—one of the most significant rituals in witchcraft. When you perform it, you are literally calling down the power of the Triple Goddess into your body. It's not a spell to be taken lightly, but it is one that can radically transform your life.

Each of these spells is completely original and is broken down in an easy-to-understand, step-by-step format. I like for my books to be easy enough for a beginner to understand but powerful enough for the experienced witch. You won't find moon magick like this anywhere else!

Night falls—are you ready to embrace the power and mystery of the moon? Then let's begin our journey!

CHAPTER 2: THE MOON PHASES

Each month, the moon moves through phases. These occur because the moon changes positions as it travels around the earth and the earth changes positions as we travel around the sun. So, as the month progresses, the moon appears to grow bigger and bigger until it is full and then smaller and smaller until it is dark.

These different phases of the moon can influence your magick in powerful ways, depending on your specific purposes. The spiritual energy of the moon aligns strongly with different types of spells at different points in the month, and as a witch you can use this to your advantage.

In this chapter, I'm going to show you the major correspondences for each phase of the moon. By learning what the current moon phase corresponds to, you can plan your magickal work at times when it will be most effective. Finally, at the end of the chapter, I'll discuss a couple rare moon events that have their own correspondences associated with them.

The New Moon

When no light from the sun is reflecting off the moon and it looks mysteriously absent from our sky, this is known as the new (or dark) moon. However, just because the moon may not be visible at this point doesn't mean it's not still working its magick!

This particular phase is a great time for banishment rituals. From ridding your mind of negative thoughts or habits to banishing bad energy from a home, this sort of magick should be saved for the new moon. The dark face of the moon during this time is charged with the power to absorb and dispel any negative spiritual forces you may be facing.

Additionally, the new moon is an appropriate time for magick meant to honor the dead or communicate with spirits. The barrier between our world and the next is at its weakest on nights when the moon doesn't shine. Always perform rituals involving the dead with the utmost caution—since this point is the time when the spiritual barrier is the weakest, it also is the time of the month when spirits are at their strongest.

The Waxing Moon

Although it begins as nothing more than a sliver, during the waxing phase of the moon it grows stronger and brighter. This is a time of new life and new beginnings, and your magick during this period should reflect that. For example, the blessing of a child, a handfasting ceremony (a Pagan wedding), or coven initiation rites should all take place during the waxing moon.

If you're a solitary practitioner, the waxing moon is also a good time to formally begin your studies. Performing an initiation or seeker ritual during this time will get your journey started on the right foot.
(If you're interested in learning more about initiation rites for solitary witches, be sure to check out my book *The Ritual Magick Manual*.)

Basically, any spells or rituals involving growth or the start of something new will benefit from the waxing moon.

The Full Moon

Most of society might associate the full moon with werewolves, but for witches, it's a bit more of a positive thing! As the moon is associated with Divine feminine power (more on that in the next chapter), this is the point in the month when the Goddess is at her peak. She is ready and willing to bestow blessings during a full moon.

As such, this is a great time for purification rituals or other blessings. The light of a full moon consecrates everything it touches, so you'll want to take advantage of it while it lasts. This can range from simply placing an object you want to bless outdoors during a full moon to a more elaborate blessing ritual, like the one we'll be looking at a little later in this book.

The full moon is also a good time for magick of protection. While the energy of the new moon banishes negativity, the energy of the full moon draws in positivity and light. Think of the moon as our celestial mother—she's watching over and protecting us from above.

Finally, fertility rites are also appropriate during the full moon. Since this is the point in the month where the spirit world is saturated with Divine feminine power, it only makes sense that this would be beneficial for childbearing.

The Waning Moon

As the moon enters the last leg of its journey, it is known as the waning moon. It's at this point it moves from bright fullness back to dark nothingness. However, this doesn't mean it's any less spiritually potent during this phase—it's simply that its energies are aligning with different types of magick.

In particular, the waning moon is the perfect time to develop your psychic or divination skills. There is much mystery and wisdom in the moon as it enters old age, so it has much to teach you. This is also the right time of the month for magick relating to dreaming or prophecy.

During the fall months, the waning moon is also a time reserved for offerings of thanksgiving to the Gods for a good harvest.

Lunar Eclipses

While they might be more common than solar eclipses, a lunar eclipse isn't something you see every day. That's why it holds particular magickal significance.

Many of the correspondences associated with the new moon are enhanced and intensified during a lunar eclipse. So, it's a particularly good time for banishment magick—especially when dealing with malevolent entities.

Really, any kind of magick involving spirits, human or otherwise, is going to be at its most potent during a total lunar eclipse. Channeling, necromancy, and exorcisms will all work well during this time. However, I urge you to proceed with extreme caution when attempting powerful rituals like these.

Finally, lunar eclipses are a good time to honor Goddesses associated with the dark of the moon. These include figures like Hecate, Tiamat, and Lilith. Although fearsome, these powerful feminine deities are at the height of their power during an eclipse and are willing to lend a hand to the worthy.

Blue Moons

In a normal year, we have 12 full moons. But from time to time, a 13th annual moon shows up. To figure out which moon during one of these years is the blue moon, you have to look at the four seasons. Typically, each season will have three full moons. When a season has four, the third moon of the season is known as the blue moon.

In more recent times, the term "blue moon" has come to refer to a month that has two full moons. While this is common usage, witches traditionally stick to the older definition of the blue moon, since it ties into the changing of the seasons and the cycle of life.

Because they're so unique, blue moons are an incredibly powerful sign of good luck. If you want to work spells that involve prosperity or material wealth, schedule them for a blue moon. You're not going to have a luckier night of the year!

CHAPTER 3: UNDERSTANDING THE TRIPLE GODDESS

The Triple Goddess is one of the most important and iconic figures in Wicca and some other forms of witchcraft. She is the primary representation of Divine feminine energy and is closely associated with the moon. So much so, in fact, that the symbol used to depict the Triple Goddess is the moon in its three primary phases—waxing, full, and waning. These three phases correspond to one of the facets or faces of the Triple Goddess. We'll talk more about them in just a little bit.

If you're serious about moon magick, it's important to get to know the Triple Goddess, because she makes appearances all over the place! In this chapter, I'm going to give you an overview of who she is, what she represents, and why she is important.

Mother, Maiden, and Crone

Like I mentioned earlier, the Triple Goddess has three facets, or faces. Each of these illuminate particular attributes associated with her. These three facets are known as the Maiden, the Mother, and the Crone. They not only represent different aspects of the Goddess, though—they also represent the different phases of life that a witch moves through.

When the moon is in its waxing phase, it's moving from the dark of the new moon to the brightness of the full moon. This phase is associated with the Maiden of the Triple Goddess.

The Maiden is depicted as a beautiful young woman, and as such, she represents qualities like purity and physical beauty. She is also a symbol of newness, life, and possibility. Think about when you were in your teen years—life stretched out in front of you, and it felt like it could lead you anywhere. Those are the feelings captured by the Maiden of the Triple Goddess.

When working magick that involves a fresh start or any kind of blessing, turn to the Maiden specifically to lend her purifying, life-giving power. Colors associated with her include springtime pastels and white (which symbolizes all Divinity). The spring equinox is a day closely associated with her, so be sure to perform some sort of ritual in her honor.

As the moon becomes full, the Maiden makes her transition into adulthood. This aspect of the Triple Goddess is known as the Mother. Like her title implies, the Mother is associated with fertility and childbirth. Her maternal nature also makes her a source of protective power for her followers.

Traditionally, witches would turn this aspect of the Triple Goddess during the harvest time to ensure that their crops grew well. But even if you're not a farmer, you can still reach out to the Mother for bounty and joy in your own life.

Moon magick centering around fertility rites, protection, or material wealth can be enhanced with help from the Mother of the Triple Goddess. Her colors include bright red, green, pink, and white. Celebrations of the Mother take place during the fall equinox, which is a time typically associated with the bounty of the harvest.

As the moon nears the end of its monthly journey, it enters the waning phase. Within the Triple Goddess, this time is represented by the Crone, or aged witch. While our society might see getting older as a bad thing, within traditional witchcraft, old age is a time of great wisdom and magick! A witch is at the height of her power as she assumes the role of the Crone.

The Crone is our primary link to the wisdom of the spiritual world. She has many lessons to teach us, thanks to her advanced age and experience. Turn to her when working magick that involves psychic abilities, prophecy, or other forms of divination. Her colors include dark red, brown, black, and white. The Crone is at the height of her power during the Winter Solstice—the time of the year when night is longest and day is shortest.

Wrapping Your Head Around the Triple Goddess

The concept of a Divine triad like this can be hard to grasp at first—she's three different things all at once, and that's something that doesn't make sense logically, on the surface at least.

However, what you've got to keep in mind is this—the Triple Goddess is a *representation* of the Divine. The Divine itself exists outside the bounds of human understanding, so we, in our finite wisdom, have to create ways to conceptualize this object of our devotion.

The Triple Goddess is simply one way that Wiccans and other witches are able to speak about the unspeakable nature of the Divine. We call her a woman and give her human attributes because that's the only way we can meaningfully discuss those aspects of the Universe that are beyond words. She's not a concept to be understood, but a force to become acquainted with.

CHAPTER 4: NEW MOON BANISHING SPELL

I t's just a fact of life that we have to deal with negative people or situations from time to time. These unpleasant encounters can drain you physically, emotionally, and spiritually, which just amplifies the bad vibes even more!

Banishing rituals are a magickal way to rid yourself of and protect yourself from negativity and bad energy that crops up in the world. They act like a spiritual force field, deflecting all the things you're trying to banish from your life.

The spell I'm going to show you in this chapter is meant for anything you might be trying to rid yourself of. Whether it's a bad habit or a difficult person, this ritual will protect you from negative influences and keep you strong when they come knocking.

Additionally, this sort of banishing magick is good for consecrating and sealing a new home. You don't need to have anything in particular that you want to banish— the ritual can protect people and places from general negativity too.

Like I mentioned in the chapter on moon phase correspondences, the new moon is the ideal time to perform a banishing ritual. Its dark face creates a sort of spiritual vacuum that can absorb bad energy and store it safely away where it can no longer influence us. So, be sure to double check your calendar to ensure that the ritual coincides with this time of the month. A banishing ritual during a new moon on a Saturday evening will be particularly powerful.

A Warning About Banishment

Before we get into the ritual itself, I want to give you a warning about banishment and the motives behind it. This type of magick should always be a means of self-defense—never perform this spell as a form of aggression towards another person.

No one wants to deal with unpleasant people, and it's perfectly reasonable to want to protect yourself from their bad influence. And this ritual can do just that. However, working magick as a way to retaliate for being treated badly is a recipe for karmic disaster. With that mindset, you're not banishing anything—you're simply redirecting the negativity towards you back out into the world.

Preparing for the Ritual

In the days leading up to the ritual, there are a few things you should do to prepare. This will ensure that your magick is at its most potent and that your banishment will be as powerful as possible.

If you have access to sage, burn some in the room after sundown for the six days before you will perform this ritual. The smoke it creates acts as a spiritual purifier that will cleanse the area of any residual negative energy—think of it like a magickal air freshener!

Additionally, a candle should burn in the room on the six evenings before the ritual. If you don't have access to lots of different colored candles, use whichever ones you have available. Ideally, you should burn a white candle (a symbol of Divine purification) the first two nights, a red candle (a symbol of will and intention) on nights three and four, and a black candle (a symbol of banishment) on the final two nights.

Below is the ritual itself.

Items Needed:
- 1 black taper candle and holder
- Matches
- Bell (the bigger the better)
- Salt (enough to make a circle around your candle)

The ritual begins by casting a sacred circle—it should be big enough to comfortably accommodate you and your supplies with plenty of room for moving around. Start at what will become the southernmost point of your circle. With your hands above your head, say this:

I cast this circle to be a place of protection. Negative energy and malevolent spirits, be gone from this hallowed ground.

Now, begin walking the circumference of your circle counterclockwise at a leisurely pace. As you walk, repeat the following:

I seal this place by the power of the dark moon.

When you return to your starting point, look outward and trace a five-pointed star (the pentagram) in the air. As you do, say the following:

Spirits of the south, keep watch over my workings.

Repeat this at each of the other cardinal directions—east, north, and west. Replace "south" in the previous invocation with whichever direction you're facing.

Move to the center of the circle and light your black candle. As you do, say:

As this light banishes darkness, so my will banishes all negativity surrounding me.

Using your salt, carefully create a complete circle around the base of your candle holder. When this is complete, say:

As this salt seals the earth, so my will seals all it touches.

Once again, walk the circumference of your circle counterclockwise, but this time, bring your bell with you. It should be rung exactly six times as you walk. After this is done, repeat:

Hear me, O spirits of protection—I call upon your power. Protect me and banish all manner of darkness and evil from my presence. Specifically, I petition that you [insert your specific banishment intention here]. Keep me safe from strife and suffering. So mote it be.

Quickly extinguish your black candle after this.

At this point, you can spend some time in meditation and contemplation, if you'd like. It's a good time to really focus your intention for the spell within your mind. Once that's done, you can formally end the ritual.

To do so, walk the circumference of your circle one final time—but this time, do it clockwise. As you walk, once again ring the bell six times. When you've made a rotation, finish up by saying:

May all who gathered here depart in peace. Though we go our separate ways, the magick we worked here remains. Blessed be.

After the work is done, dispose of the salt outdoors. This ritual is powerful, but it won't last forever. If you are still seeking banishment after six months, consider repeating it again.

CHAPTER 5: FULL MOON BLESSING SPELL

The blessing spell I'm about to show you acts as a counterpoint to the banishing ritual in the last chapter. While the former was all about keeping bad energy out, this one is all about brining good energy in.

And there's no better time than a full moon to seek out the positive energy of the universe! Its bright rays have purifying spiritual properties than can cleanse spaces, objects, or even people. Since the full moon is associated with the Divine feminine, we'll be invoking her purifying power as well.

Blessing Spell Uses

I've kept this spell intentionally broad so that you can adapt it to your specific needs. Basically, if you have something that needs blessing, you can probably fit it into the structure I provide you. However, this ritual is particularly good for consecrating a new home, blessing your witchcraft tools, or surrounding yourself and others with positive energy.

Items Needed:
- 1 white taper candle and holder
- Matches
- Small bouquet of flowers (hand-picked is best)
- 1 gold ribbon (long enough to tie around the bouquet)

As always, you'll begin by casting a sacred circle. To do this, stand at the northernmost point and light your white candle. Slowly begin walking clockwise around the outline of your circle with your candle. As you do so, repeat this:

This circle is open and welcomes all spirits of goodwill. Let us gather by the light of the full moon and receive its blessings.

After making a single round, place your white candle back down at the northernmost point of your circle.

Move to the center of your circle, where your flowers and ribbon should be waiting. Pick up the flowers and hold them above your head—if your space allows it, try to place them somewhere where the light of the moon can touch them.

As you hold them, say:

Great mother Goddess of the moon, this is my offering to you. May you imbue these flowers with your Divine power and protection. May they serve as a beacon of your blessings.

Now, take the gold ribbon and tie them around the stems of the bouquet. If you're handy with knots, use a square knot to tie it (as this has spiritual symbolism in witchcraft). Otherwise, tie it in a bow or some other knot. Once this is completed, you should now say:

I seal this icon with the Divine power of gold. May no one and nothing undo the blessing it contains.

If you have specific objects or people you want to bless, continue on with the ritual from here. Otherwise, skip to the end of this spell.

To bless an object or person with the bouquet, hold it with both hands in front of the object of your blessing. Trace the shape of a five-pointed star (known as a pentagram) in the air and repeat these words:

I seal this [person/object] with the Divine power of the holy Goddess, our lunar mother. May her power be present and always working good within [you/it].

The previous blessing can be repeated as many times as necessary.

To conclude the ritual, place the bouquet back at the center of the circle, raise your hands above your head, and give this farewell to the Goddess:

Divine Goddess of the full moon, our work is complete. Thank you for your power and protection. May we depart in peace to meet again soon. So mote it be.

Return to your white candle and pick up. Make one final trip around your circle—but this time, it should be counterclockwise. As you walk, repeat the following:

Although we depart, our magick remains. May all within this circle return to their homes in peace and safety. So mote it be.

The ritual will officially end when you extinguish your white candle.

If this ritual was used to bless people or objects, you can dispose of your bouquet outdoors immediately. It should not be reused for future blessings.

If this ritual was for the blessing of a home or room, the flowers should be kept within the space for three days. On the evening of the third day, the flowers should be disposed of outdoors.

CHAPTER 6: WAXING MOON SPELL FOR A FRESH START

W e all find ourselves in a rut from time to time. The routines of everyday life become a burden, and it seems like we lose that spark for life that we once had. If you find yourself trapped in the same old, same old and are ready to start truly living again, you're in need of a fresh start. And wouldn't you know—I have just the moon spell for that!

When the moon is in the waxing phase, it's still in the infancy of its monthly journey. During this time, the energies corresponding to life, vitality, and newness are at their peak, so there's no better occasion to start a new chapter in your life.

This fresh start ritual is meant to be a formal way of dedicating yourself to making a change. It's a way of telling the universe loud and clear, "This is the first day of the rest of my life."

Whether you're looking for a career change, want to become more social, or simply need to hit the reset button on life, you can harness the power of the waxing moon to start your new journey on the right foot. It's as simple as asking for a little help from the spirit world!

The ritual should (obviously) be performed during a waxing moon, which lasts about 12 to 13 days. Unlike spells involving a full moon (which only lasts one night), you have a little more wiggle room when planning waxing moon magick. If possible, schedule the night of your ritual specifically on a Monday, as its energies work well in conjunction with those of the waxing moon.

Items Needed:
- Small bowl filled with water
- 1 white or silver taper candle and holder
- Matches
- 1 piece of silver ribbon

Before the ritual begins, allow your bowl of water to sit under the light of the waxing moon for thirty minutes to an hour. This will charge the water with the sacred energy that the moon bestows us. This energy can then be transferred to anything the water touches.

Begin by casting a sacred circle. To do this, light your silver candle and begin at the northernmost point of your space. Walk a circle around your ritual space (clockwise), and as you do, repeat this:

I open this circle as the moon begins her celestial journey. May her radiance bless all it touches with newness of body, mind, and spirit.

Return to the northernmost point and place the candle there.

Now, go to the center of your circle with the blessed water. Hold it with both hands above your head and say:

The blessings of the moon are contained in this sacred vessel. All that it touches will be washed clean with the purifying power of light.

At this point, you have a few options. If you want, you can place your hands into the bowl and splash water over your entire face. If that's not a realistic option for you, dip your right index finger into the water and use it to draw a circle of water on your forehead. The point here is to symbolize your fresh start through the use of water— do whatever feels comfortable and appropriate to you.

After this, say the following:

I am sealed with the power of the waxing moon. My new journey awaits me. [Here you can add some personalized information about your own unique fresh start.] May the Triple Goddess, our celestial mother, watch over me every step of the way. So mote it be.

Now, take your silver ribbon and tie three knots in it. These don't have to be perfect, but try to space them as evenly as possible.

This small object is a symbol of the Triple Goddess and is meant to act as both a reminder and talisman for you. Every time you look at it, you will be encouraged to remember your intention to start anew—this will come in handy when the going gets tough and you're tempted to toss out your plans for life. However, this object is also imbued with the energy of the moon, so it will continue to draw in its refreshing power long after the ritual is over.

With the knots tied, hold the ribbon in your hands and say:

Behold the sign of the Triple Goddess.

Take a small amount of water with your right index finger and anoint the ribbon with it. As you do, repeat:

May these sacred knots bind the power of the moon to themselves. May they bless all in their presence.

To end your ritual, return to your silver candle and pick it up. This time, walk a counterclockwise circle around your space to dissolve the sacred circle. As you walk, say:

Though the circle opens, may the Divine Goddess of the moon continue to watch over me on my journey. With her help, I can walk this path with courage. So mote it be.

Extinguish the candle to formally end the spell.

After the ritual, try to keep the knotted ribbon on you at all times. Like I said, it serves as a reminder of your intention, but it also draws spiritual energy into itself that will help you along the way. Your water should be disposed of outdoors.

By Didi Clarke

CHAPTER 7: WANING MOON DREAM SPELL

Spiritual insight and wisdom don't operate like traditional wisdom. If you want to learn a practical skill, you read a book about it or find someone to teach it to you. And while books and teachers are an important part of witchcraft, true wisdom comes from a direct encounter with the spirit world itself—through things like divination, astral projection, and, in our case, dreams.

Dreams are a strange, mysterious thing—even modern science can't seem to figure out exactly what they are or why we developed the ability to dream! However, what we in the world of witchcraft do know about dreams is this: they are the place where the rational mind and the murky depths of the subconscious meet. And since the subconscious mind has a much stronger connection to the spirit world, it is our key to unlocking the esoteric wisdom of this place.

When we dream, our minds are filled with highly symbolic images that don't make much sense on a rational level. This is because dreams are messages from the spirit world. Unfortunately, our highly logical human brains have difficulty understanding the language of the Divine. So, these messages have to be translated into a language we understand.

Dreams take these messages and translate them into things we can wrap our heads around. Unlocking the symbols within dreams and how they relate to one another can be a challenge, but each of us has an innate sense of what the spirit world is trying to tell us—even if we don't always realize it. Through developing this intuition (and plenty of practice!) anyone can become adept at interpreting and understanding the language of dreams.

Dreams and the Moon

Within the monthly cycle of the moon, the energy associated with prophetic or significant dreams is highest during the waning phase—the time when the moon moves from being full back into the dark nothingness of the new moon. All kinds of psychic abilities are enhanced at this time on the calendar, but dreams are especially enhanced because of their connection with sleep, which is obviously connected to nighttime and the moon.

Like I mentioned in the chapter on the Triple Goddess, the waning moon is associated with the Crone—the wise, aged witch who is happy to share the spirit wisdom she has accumulated through her years of experience. So, in this dream ritual, I'll show you how to petition the Crone for important messages via dreams. These messages you'll be asking for can be about a specific problem you're dealing with, but you can also ask more generally for the wisdom that she thinks will benefit your life in a positive way.

The Dream Ritual

Below, I'll show you the ritual itself first, and then I'll follow up with some tips you can use to enhance your dreaming even more. There's definitely an art to remembering and interpreting your dreams, and these techniques will help you to enhance your craft.

Items Needed:
- 1 white or silver taper candle and holder
- Lavender incense and holder
- Matches
- Small, polished black stone

Begin by lighting your candle and creating a sacred circle. To do so, hold the candle while you walk a clockwise circle around your space. As you walk, repeat the following:

I open the space where spirit and mortal meet. It is a world of dreams and wisdom.

Place your candle at the center of your circle. Now, light your incense and make another lap around your space while saying:

I anoint this space with the scent of mystic wisdom. Within the haze lies the answer I seek.

Place your incense to the right of the candle. Next, while standing in front of the candle with both hands raised to the sky, invoke the Crone with this prayer:

Wise Crone, I call your power into this sacred circle. You alone hold the keys to the wisdom of the spirit world. Unlock my mind and soul, that I may share in your knowledge through the power of dreams. Your knowledge is needed to illuminate the path of my life. Specifically, I seek guidance about [here is where you can personalize your request for advice]. If I am worthy, meet me in my dreams.

To continue the prayer, pick up your stone and say this:

May this stone serve as the point of our communion. Fill it with your power that it may influence and affect my dreams whenever I am in its presence.

At this point, the ritual itself is nearly done—although the actual work of dreaming has yet to begin! To conclude, pick up your candle and extinguish it. Afterwards, repeat this:

Though we depart the sacred circle, great Crone, may we visit again soon in the realm of dreams.

After the Ritual

There are a few things you should do after the ritual to ensure you remember your dreams as clearly as possible.

First, make sure that the small stone from the ritual is somewhere in your room every night when you go to bed. Ideally, it should be placed under your mattress, but if that's not a possibility, place it on your nightstand or a shelf. This stone is now imbued with the power of the Crone, and the energy it emanates will help you to remember and understand your dreams.

Next, try to burn some incense before bed every night. I would recommend using lavender like in the ritual, as it corresponds to divination and the spirit world in general.

Finally, keep a dream journal. It is an indispensable tool for anyone who wants to remember and interpret their dreams. Keep it by your bedside and jot down any dreams you have the moment you wake up. Even if you can't remember the whole thing, write down any snippets, impressions, or images you do remember. Over time, your dream journal will help train your brain to better remember your dreams upon waking. It's also a good way to track recurring themes, symbols, or people who crop up in your dreams over and over again.

Once you've performed the ritual, you may have to wait a bit before the dreams start coming—the spirit world moves on its own time, not ours. However, when performed correctly, rest assured that this ritual will ensure your messages from the Divine   are   on   their   way

CHAPTER 8: SELENE INVOCATION

Selene is a Greek Goddess that is often incorporated into the Triple Goddess as the Mother. Although she is commonly depicted as overwhelmingly beautiful and fair, looks can be deceiving! This Goddess is a powerful maternal figure and a source of inner strength for the many witches that call upon her. While other deities associated with the moon are seen as fearsome and aggressive, Selene is an exception. Her power comes not from brute displays of force, but through her gentle, enveloping radiance. Her protection is a source of comfort to her followers.

Because of her status as the Mother, you will often see Selene incorporated into rituals about fertility, pregnancy, and childbirth. Dedicating a child to Selene is a way to ensure that he or she will be cared for and watched over their entire life. And while she is no doubt a powerful symbol of new life, that's not all Selene is known for.

This celestial Goddess is also a favorite of astrologers and others that watch the stars. You can turn to Selene for guidance about the best times and days for performing a spell based on the positions of all the celestial bodies—because she is symbolized the moon, she rules as queen over all the night sky and the stars and planets it contains.

However, even if you're not particularly astrologically inclined, Selene can still be a source of guidance and wisdom in everyday life. In fact, the ritual I'll show you a little bit later in this chapter is all about petitioning Selene for advice about major obstacles or changes.

Selene Correspondences

Certain colors, objects, and symbols are particularly powerful when used to invoke Selene. These are known as correspondences, since they correspond well with her spiritual energies.

Like all deities, white is Selene's primary color. White candles, white flowers, white ribbons, etc. all will enhance your intentions when working with her. In particular, white lilies are a good choice for an offering to Selene.

However, because of her status as a moon Goddess, silver is another powerful color to incorporate into your rituals involving Selene. If possible, perform the following ritual under the silver rays of the moon itself. Because she is associated with the Mother in the Triple Goddess, the full moon is the best time to invoke Selene, but really, your spellwork involving her will be enhanced by the presence of the moon at any phase.

Selene Flame Gazing Ritual

Like I mentioned earlier, Selene is a Divine companion most willing to give advice and guidance to her followers. In this ritual, I'll show you how to invoke the Goddess using the flame of a candle. By gazing gently into its flicker, Selene will begin to show you glimpses of the path that you should take.

This spell can be used for guidance of all kinds. It works if you've got a decision to make and are torn between two choices, but it's also useful when you're in a tough situation and don't even know where to begin! Selene is open and free with her advice to all—if only we would ask.

(Author's Note: A version of this ritual originally appeared in my book *Forbidden Wiccan Spells Vol. 3: Dark Goddess Magick.* I've made some changes to the spell since then, but I would highly recommend trying out both versions for yourself and seeing which one works better for you.)

Items Needed:
- 1 silver taper candle and holder
- Floral incense (choose a scent that's pleasing to you) and holder
- Matches
- 1 white lily (or other white flower)

Begin by clearing a space to cast a sacred circle. Stand at the northernmost point with your white lily in your right hand. Begin to walk a clockwise circle around your space while you repeat this:

This circle opens for the honor of the Goddess Selene. Watch over my workings, sacred moon mother.

Once you've made a complete circle, place the white lily at the center of your space. Now, pick up and light your incense. Once again, make a clockwise circle around your space while you say:

I prepare this space for the Divine. As the smoke rises, so it purifies everything it touches. This place is worthy of the great Goddess.

After this is finished, place the incense at the northernmost point of your circle.

Next we come to the invocation to Selene herself. Light your silver candle at the center of your space and place your hands palms-up in the air. Say the following with authority and conviction:

I call the lunar Goddess Selene down from the heavens. I have prepared this space for your pleasure. I call out to you, wise Goddess, for you alone know the mysteries of the stars. Guide me in your Divine knowledge that I might make prudent choices. Specifically, I petition you for knowledge about [here is where you explain your issue or decision]. With your guiding hand, may I choose the path that's right for me.

Now, take some time to gaze into the light of the flame. Don't overthink things—allow yourself to become hypnotized by its flicker. Push everything else out of your mind except for this singular flame.

As you gaze longer, glimpses or small flashes of thoughts may begin to pop up unexpectedly. This is Selene trying to make herself known. In the moment, don't worry about interpreting the messages you're receiving from her—that comes later. For now, just do your best to take in everything she is bestowing upon you.

When the flashes die down and your mind begins to quiet, it's time to end the ritual. Start by thanking Selene for her presence. To do this, say:

Mother of the stars, your wisdom has been made known to me. Let us depart in love and peace, with the hope that we will meet again soon. It is through your knowledge that I thrive.

Now, extinguish your candle.

Finally, you need to open your sacred circle. To do so, pick up the white lily again (this time in your left hand) and walk around your space counterclockwise. As you do, repeat this:

The circle opens and we depart, but the magick worked here remains forever. So mote it be.

After the ritual is over, be sure to dispose of your rose outdoors.

Interpreting the messages you get from Selene can be tricky—Gods and Goddesses rarely speak straightforwardly to humans, so the visions you received are likely to be highly symbolic and coded.

Write down everything you can remember from the ritual and give yourself plenty of time to work through what you've recorded. Acting too quickly and rashly with information you've been given by the Divine can often have more devastating consequences than acting with no information at all! Have the confidence and patience to know that, in due time, Selene's message will make sense to you.

CHAPTER 9: HECATE INVOCATION

Hecate is another Greek Goddess that is commonly associated with the Triple Goddess—she occupies the role of the Crone. Unlike Selene, who is depicted at maternal and inviting, Hecate is downright fearsome in her depictions. This probably has a lot to do with the fact that she oversees the realms of the dead, necromancy, and black magick.

It's true that she's associated with some heavy subjects, but death and the great beyond are not things that a witch should fear—they are simply one stage in the never-ending cycle of life, death, and rebirth. As a gatekeeper between the living and the dead, Hecate has much to teach us about the spirit world.

And so we turn to Hecate just as we would turn to Selene or any other manifestation of the Triple Goddess—for understanding and growth. And just because she's a little rough around the edges doesn't mean that Hecate isn't protective and maternal! That's one trait shared by all Goddesses associated with the moon.

Hecate Correspondences

As a deity, the color white can be used with Hecate, but this is one instance where making an exception to this rule is probably a good idea—black seems like a much more natural fit for her, considering that she corresponds to the new or dark moon.

Candles are a must when working with Hecate, too. They symbolize the torches her ancient Greek followers would have used to illuminate their rituals to her in the dead of night.

Her animal familiars include ravens, owls, bats, and wolves—all creatures associated with darkness and immense magickal power.

Belladonna, hemlock, mandrake, and poppies are all plants that amplify the power of Hecate. However, many of these plants are dangerous both magickally and physically, so use caution when including them in your rituals.

Hecate Ritual for Spirit Communion

This ritual emphasizes Hecate's role as a gatekeeper between this world and the next. With it, you will be able to make psychic contact with Spirits, all mediated by this powerful and watchful Goddess.

Caution: working with ghosts is not a matter to take lightly. Hecate can provide you with protection and guidance, but only if you approach her respectfully and correctly. Familiarize yourself intimately with this ritual before attempting, and be absolutely sure that Spirit contact is something you truly desire.

Items needed:
- 4 white candles
- 1 black candle
- Bowl of water
- Salt
- White ribbon (enough to tie around your wrist)

Place the four white candles at each of the four cardinal directions and light them in this order: east, west, north, south. As you light them, repeat the following:

Dark Goddess Hecate, guide me and protect me as I journey into the realm of night. You are my keeper.

Return to the center of the circle and face south—since we're dealing with ghosts, it makes sense to face the "direction" of the Underworld. Take your white ribbon and tie it around your wrist. This is simply another precaution to keep your safe. As you tie, say:

Bound to light, bound to goodness. Keep me safe along the dark path.

Next, you will need to ritually cleanse yourself with the water before proceeding. Place your hands over the bowl and imagine white light emanating from it. Dip your right index finger into the water and swipe it across your forehead, right to left. As you do, say:

Pure mind, pure intention.

Next, dip your finger in the water again. This time, make a swipe across your heart while saying:

Pure heart, pure intention.

Finally, dip your finger once more and swipe across your left palm. Say:

Pure will, pure intention.

Now is the time to invoke Hecate. Light the black candle, raise your hands over your head, and repeat the following:

Great crone Hecate, queen of the night, I beg your assistance. Enter this sacred circle that it may become a portal to those long gone. You are the wise and powerful gatekeeper of the dead. Only allow those whose intentions are as pure as mine to enter this hallowed ground. Mother Hecate, bring the vision of Spirits into my mind's eye. Let them speak.

Close your eyes and allow the silence to wash over you. If you have a particular Spirit you would like to speak to, visualize that person in your mind. If not, try to clear your head of all thought.

It may take some time at first, but eventually, you will begin to get "glimpses" of messages in your mind. Allow the Spirits to enter and speak with as little interference from your conscious mind as possible.

These messages may be confusing or surreal, but don't let that bother you. The point now is to simply be a conduit for these ghosts to communicate. Pondering their message will come later after the ritual.

When you are satisfied with the messages you have received, it's time to seal the portal and end the ritual. I cannot emphasize this enough: do not skip this part. While you may have only allowed ghosts access to this world via the psychic realm, less friendly Spirits may exploit your generosity in more physical, tangible ways if you leave the portal open too long.

To complete the ritual, begin by saying the following:

Great Hecate, the will is accomplished. Seal this portal that none may pass through again.

Next, you need to thank and release Hecate from the circle. Extinguish the black candle and repeat:

Spiritual mother, spiritual guide, I thank you and bless you for your presence. Depart now and leave this realm in peace. Your generosity will not soon be forgotten.

Now, extinguish the white candles in this order: south, north, west, east. At each candle, say the following:

The night is over, the day is coming. May all who gathered in this circle depart in friendship.

The black candle can be used again, but only for future rituals involving Hecate. If possible, wrap it in a nice cloth and store it somewhere safe as a symbol of reverence to this awesome Goddess.

CHAPTER 10: ESBAT CELEBRATION

Within the year, there are eight major holidays observed by witches and Wiccans, and these are known as Sabbats. However, these are not the only important days on the magickal calendar—the full moon during every month is another time for celebration, and this celebration is known as an esbat. Basically, it's a time we set aside to honor the Triple Goddess and celebrate the beauty, wonder, and mystery of the moon.

Unlike the more serious, solemn ceremony of Drawing Down the Moon (which also takes place during a full moon), an esbat is more of a time for fun and merrymaking. Magickal spells and rituals can still absolutely factor into your observance, but the mood is much lighter. In fact, the term "esbat" comes from the French term *s'ebattre*, which means to amuse or entertain oneself.

Since the occasion does deal primarily with the Divine, we do try to be respectful. But being respectful doesn't mean we can't honor the Goddess with joy and laughter. An esbat is a time for smiles, not scowls.

In this chapter, I'll show you everything you need to know in order to celebrate the esbats with witchy style! From altar decorations to invocations and prayers you can use, you'll be fully prepared by the time the next full moon comes around.

Traditionally, esbat celebrations are an important time for members of a coven to spend time with one another, but a solitary witch can absolutely celebrate these important days too. All of my suggestions, ideas, and tips can be modified to include one or more people, depending on your own personal situation.

Esbat Decorations

Now, I'm an arts and crafts-type witch at heart, which means that I absolutely love decorating my altar and home any chance I get. But don't feel like you have to throw together every single décor tip I send your way—while you should do at least a little something to spruce up your magickal space on the full moon, you don't have to be as extravagant as you would be when celebrating a Sabbat. That being said, if you're a creative type too, by all means throw on all the bells and whistles!

For a simple décor idea, try some colored candles. My personal preference is for a large, silver candle embellished with a pink ribbon bow. The silver candle represents the full moon and the spiritual energy that emanates from it, while the pink bow is simply a bright, striking representation of the joy that should accompany an esbat celebration.

I've also seen some witches get creative with a candle-based representation of the Triple Goddess—a white candle for the Maiden, a silver candle for the Mother, and a black candle for the Crone. While an esbat does technically take place on a full moon (associated with the Mother), I think it's a great idea to try and incorporate the other aspects of the Triple Goddess as well.

An esbat is also the right time to pull out anything silver or white colored that you might have—altar cloths, table runners, gemstones, robes, etc. This is a night for honoring both the moon and the Divine, so both of these colors will be welcome additions.

If you're a lover of all things floral, a nice bouquet of flowers can spruce up your altar for an esbat too. Poppies are a strong symbol of Divine presence, so they could be a good choice, but personally, I prefer to choose a flower that's in season depending on the time of year. It's just another way I feel I can tap into the natural rhythm of nature.

If possible, also try to arrange your celebration space near a window. We can throw together all the fancy, complicated decorations we want, but when it comes down to it, all we need is the pure light of the full moon for the perfect esbat ceremony.

Esbat Rituals

Incorporating the Triple Goddess into your festivities is one way to celebrate an esbat. However, you need to keep in mind that this is more of a time for honoring the Goddess, as opposed to petitioning her for something. So, your prayers and invocations should center around this.

For a short and sweet invocation to begin your esbat celebration, try this:

Great mother Goddess, queen of the Moon—join us with joy and laughter in this place. Tonight we celebrate you in your goodness and wisdom. As we turn to you, turn to us in the Divine communion of peace and happiness. So mote it be.

Author's note: "We" and "us" in the previous invocation can be altered to "I" and "me" for solitary witches.

For a longer ceremony, try this ritual blessing of the Triple Goddess. It's particularly suited for use in a group setting, but it can be performed alone with a few modifications.

Before the ritual, fill a bowl with water and allow it to sit under the light of the full moon for at least 30 minutes.

To begin the ritual, the coven High Priestess (or appointed ritual leader) should say the following:

We gather tonight under the Divine light of the full moon to honor the great Triple Goddess that sustains us. Join us, our lunar companion, in the joy of our celebration.

The large silver candle should be lit by the ritual leader, while the other esbat attendees hold their smaller candles as well. As the large candle is lit, the leader says:

The eternal light of the Triple Goddess burns within our hearts and illuminates the darkness.

Now, the leader turns to the person on their right and lights their candle with the larger one. As the new candle is lit, the leader says:

May the blessings of the full moon make your heart glad.

Next, this person should turn to the attendee on their right and light their candle while repeating:

May the blessings of the full moon make your heart glad.

This process should repeat until everyone in the circle has their candle lit.

At this point, the leader should step into the middle of the circle and say the following:

Come, let us share in the blessings of the great Goddess.

Next, the leader should pick up the bowl of water and move in front of the person who was standing to their right. The leader should dip their right thumb into the water and use it to draw a circle in the person's forehead. After this is complete, the leader should say:

I seal you with the power of the Triple Goddess.

The leader should continue down the line until every attendee has been sealed. At this point, the leader should return to the center of the circle and say:

We are all one within the Divine light of the moon. May we share in its joy and peace until we meet again. So mote it be.

Esbats are also a time to reflect on the previous month and make plans for the coming one. So, in addition to these two specific rituals, any sort of magick that involves goals or aspirations make a welcome addition to an esbat celebration.

CHAPTER 11: BLUE MOON RITUAL

Blue moons are not a common occurrence—they show up on average once every two to three years. And while we'll all probably see several in our lives, the sightings will be few and far between. Because of their relative rarity, blue moons are a powerful sign of good luck or unexpected prosperity.

Like I mentioned in the chapter on moon phases, a blue moon occurs when a season has four full moons (as opposed to the normal three), and the blue moon in particular is the third moon of that season. Some people consider a blue moon to be a second full moon in a calendar month, but witches typically prefer the more traditional definition

So when is the next blue moon? It's either very soon or very far away—depending on who you ask! Here are the next six upcoming blue moons (using the more traditional definition):

August 22, 2021
August 19, 2024
May 20, 2027
August 24, 2029
August 21, 2032
May 22, 2035

Why is it Called a Blue Moon?

If you look up into the sky on the night of a blue moon, can you expect to see our lunar friend literally tinged blue? Probably not.

Strangely enough, it appears that the term "blue moon" actually originates from Christianity and the early-modern English term "belewe", which means "to betray."

Within Western Christianity, the date for Easter is calculated as the Sunday after the first full moon after the spring equinox. So, the faithful could expect that their fasting (which is traditionally performed in the weeks leading up to Easter) would soon come to an end when this full moon appeared.

However, if the spring contained four full moons instead of three, this blue moon "betrayed" their expectation about the end of the fast. And over time, this term, "belewe moon" morphed (intentionally or unintentionally) into "blue moon."

There are technically times when the moon does actually appear blue in hue. But this is not a sign of good luck—it's a sign that a natural disaster has taken place. When particles of a certain size enter the atmosphere, they have the ability to scatter the red light reflected by the moon, making it appear to glow blue. The most common source of particles this size are, unfortunately, volcanic eruptions and wildfires.

Blue Moon Spells

The following are a few simple, quick spells you can try out the next time a blue moon rolls around. And don't worry—you've got plenty of time to practice before that happens!

Mint for Luck

Mint is an herb that is strongly associated with luck and serendipity. Carry a mint leaf around in your wallet or purse and see if the universe sends a happy accident your way!

Charging a Good Luck Charm

People from cultures across the globe use good luck charms in one form or another. From a lucky rabbit's foot to a four-leaf clover, there are no shortage of small (and large!) objects that we use to attract good luck.

If you've got a good luck charm that's personal to you, a blue moon is the perfect time to infuse it with the energy of that lucky night. Allow it to sit overnight in direct moonlight to experience the full effect of the moon's power.

Prayer to Fortuna

Fortuna is a Roman Goddess associated with luck and destiny. She is the deity you should turn to if you want the winds of fortune to blow your way. This short prayer to her can be used to petition for her favor.

But be sure to bring an offering with you! If you don't show her the proper reverence, she may decide not to bestow a blessing upon you. Fresh flowers or a bundle of mint leaves both make an appropriate offering, but don't be afraid to get creative and think of something else that's thoughtful and meaningful.

The prayer goes like this:

Mistress Fortuna, I call to thee. May my offering bring me favor in your eyes. By your hand the wheel of fortune spins. Move me upward, that I may abide closer to thee. Grant me good fortune and peaceful days. Blessed be.

CHAPTER 12: DRAWING DOWN THE MOON

D rawing down the Moon is arguably the most sacred, powerful ritual we have that involves the moon. It is the event where human and Divinity meet in a direct encounter with one another—the Triple Goddess descends to enter the soul of the one who calls Her.

This is not a practice to take lightly by any means—contact with the Divine requires respect and preparation. And this isn't your typical invocation. You're not calling the Goddess into your sacred space, you're calling the Goddess directly into your inner being. For those who have experienced this sacred communion firsthand, it is the event of a lifetime. It reconnects us to the spiritual world in a way that no other magick can.

Why Draw Down the Moon?

Witches have been Drawing down the Moon for ages—we believe the ritual began in ancient Thessaly (which is a part of Greece) with practitioners in the second century BCE. Since then, the process has been passed down from generation to generation until it evolved into the rite we know today.

Aside from tradition, why do we still go to all this trouble? Drawing down the Moon demands much physically, emotionally, and spiritually from a witch, but what does she receive in return?

Most importantly, Drawing down the Moon puts us in direct connection with the Divine. Until we pass beyond this life into the next, we have very few opportunities to experience an immediate, all-encompassing encounter with the universal Divine spirit. Drawing down the Moon is an occasion for a very rare, sacred event, and that explains much of its appeal.

Additionally, Drawing down the Moon is a means for communicating directly with the Triple Goddess. We make prayers to the Goddess and seek out signs of her presence in our lives, but within this ritual, she speaks to us directly. Within a coven setting, the High Priestess will invoke the Triple Goddess into herself and, for a time, become her mouthpiece here on earth. However, solitary witches can still perform this ritual and speak with the Goddess personally, not as a vessel.

Preparing for the Ritual

Preparation for any ritual is important, but let's be honest—we all skimp on it from time to time, don't we? Sometimes we can get away with it, but when it comes to Drawing down the Moon, it's essential to be prepared. The ritual can be such a beautiful, moving experience that you don't want anything to get in the way of that beauty.

First up is the timing. Traditionally, the ritual is performed on a full moon. I know some witches who perform it at other times, but I would very highly personally recommend the full moon. This is supposed to be a complete encounter with the Divine, so it makes sense to wait until the moon is at its most complete.

Additionally, this is a ritual that really needs to be performed outside under the light of the full moon. If that is just a complete impossibility for you, indoors is acceptable. But I really do implore you to try and find a way to Draw down the Moon outside.

On the day of the ritual, try to give yourself some time between Drawing down the Moon and the rest of life. Don't go straight from a long day at work right into the ritual! Give yourself an hour or so before and after the ritual to really appreciate its full effects. Use the time before to focus and center your thoughts, and use the time after to reflect on what you've experienced.

You might also consider taking a ritual bath to purify and cleanse yourself beforehand. There are more elaborate rituals you can try for this (see my book *The Ritual Magick Manual* for a short bathing ritual). However, a typical bath with a few drops of your favorite essential oil is just fine too. As you bathe, imagine the water filled with bright, white light that cleanses your spirit as well as your body.

Finally, I would also suggest a "dress rehearsal" version of this ritual. Walk yourself through the process step-by-step (without actually saying the words or performing the actions) just to ensure that you understand the flow of the ritual. There's nothing worse than being caught off guard right in the middle of a spell unfolding!

Drawing Down the Moon Ritual

My version of this ritual requires no items. When you Draw down the Moon, your body is the only tool you need.

To begin with, stand in the center of your space with your eyes closed. Your hands should be at your side, with the palms facing forward. The opening invocation is based on the lines that the ancient witches of Thessaly recited during the ritual:

I stand before the holy moon. My intention is the whole of my being. At my command, land, sea, and air bend to my will. This sacred night lingers until I release it to the day.

Next, move to a kneeling position on the floor. If you wish, you can move to a full prostration, with your forehead touching the floor and your arms stretched out in front of you. Continue the ritual:

Great Goddess of the night sky, I bow before your presence. Within your Divine light, my will is perfected, my intention is brought into line with your providence. I bid you welcome.

Return to the standing and move to the northernmost point in your space. Say this:

Spirits of the north, watch and keep silence as the Sacred Lady draws near.

Now, move to the south:

Spirits of the south, watch and keep silence as the Sacred Lady draws near.

Next, the west:

Spirits of the west, watch and keep silence as the Sacred Lady draws near.

Finally, the east:

Spirits of the east, watch and keep silence as the Sacred Lady draws near.

Return to the center of your space and raise your arms outstretched above your head. In a loud and confident voice, say this:

Hail to the Triple Goddess who bears many faces and many names. Your servant is here to receive you. Mother, Maiden, Crone, here am I, your vessel. The time of communion is upon us. I call you from the heavens down into my soul. Welcome, O great and fearsome woman!

At this point, the spirit of the Divine enters your body. People react to this experience in different ways. Some people experience as it a feeling of active, chaotic ecstasy. Others experience a deep, meditative trance. Allow your body to react how it may and for as long as it may.

During this time, you will be in direct communion with the Triple Goddess. You can speak to her in your mind, you can speak to her out loud, or you can allow her to give a message through you. This may sound a little scary, but be brave! The Goddess has accepted you as her vessel, which is an extremely high honor. And as our celestial mother, she certainly means you no harm.

When it's time for this communion to end, you'll know in your heart. There isn't a set amount of time that this ritual should last, but if it's coming to a close, you'll know intuitively.

Begin to bring your mind back up into a normal state of consciousness. Don't rush yourself through this process—depending on your encounter, mild disorientation can occur as you move back up into full awareness. This is not dangerous and is completely temporary, but it can happen, since this sort of Divine contact is so out of the ordinary.

When you're ready to conclude, return to a kneeling position, with your hands raised above your head. Repeat this:

I have known the Divine mother within my very essence. I am changed forever and irrevocably. May this night fill the whole world with the sacred peace I have just encountered. Blessed Goddess of the moon, with my love I bid you farewell. I am your servant in word and deed, help me to spread your blessings far and wide. Let us depart in peace to meet again in love. So mote it be.

Like I mentioned earlier, after this ritual is complete, give yourself some time to recuperate and recharge before returning to life as usual. While this ritual can be performed at every full moon, it is a very demanding spell, so I only recommend using it once every season at the most.

CHAPTER 13: EMBRACE THE DIVINE MOON

As witches, when we look into the night sky, we don't just see the moon—we see the Divine. Every night, our celestial mother rises to keep watch over us and bless us with the power of her gentle light. For a witch, there is nothing more sacred or beautiful than this scene.

It's my hope that this book hasn't just shown you how to tap into the magickal power of the moon, but also why it is such an important and comforting force in our lives. The moon isn't just some natural resource waiting to be exploited, nor is it some dead, cold stone floating in the nothingness of space. It is alive with the energy of the spirit world and it calls us into a relationship with the Divine itself.

If you enjoyed what you read, please consider signing up for my email list. You'll be notified every time I publish a new book or have something exciting in the works. When you sign up, you'll also receive a free color magick correspondence chart that's perfect for enhancing your spellwork spiritually and visually! Use the following link to find the sign-up page: https://mailchi.mp/01863952b9ff/didi-clarke-mailing-list

Additionally, I would be extremely grateful for an honest review of the book. I want to provide my readers with spells and magickal rituals that are important and useful to them, and receiving your feedback is one way I can better serve you.

Blessed Be,

Didi

CHAPTER 14: READ MORE FROM DIDI CLARKE

Forbidden Wiccan Spells: Magick for Love and Power (Vol. 1)

Enchant your way to romance with these Wiccan love spells! Become a master of power magick! Learn all this and much more with this original spell book from Didi Clarke!

Whether you're trying to seduce that special someone or want to show others who's the boss, *Forbidden Wiccan Spells: Magick for Love and Power* has something for everyone. With each chapter, you'll find authentic Wiccan magic that will help you unlock your dreams in love and life!

What You'll Find

Within the pages of *Magick for Love and Power*, you'll find one-of-a-kind spells written and tested by Didi Clarke herself—you won't find books on witchcraft like this anywhere else!

If you're new to Wicca, never fear—this book uses a wicca for beginners approach. The spells are explained thoroughly, and each one comes with a detailed item list and step-by-step directions.

And there's plenty for more experienced witches too. These unique magick rituals will enhance your skills and help you tap into the full potential of love and power! In this book, you'll find a wide variety of magickal practices to explore, including:

- Herbal Magick
- Candle Magick
- Mantra Magick
- Elemental Magick

Are you ready to spice up your life with love spells?

Love is a powerful force, and when you combine it with the power of witchcraft, the results can be truly magickal! In *Magick for Love and Power*, you'll get access to genuine spells and rituals that will help you attract romance into your life and keep the flames of love burning for years to come!

These love spells include:

- Flame gazing to find your true love
- Mantras to keep your partner faithful
- Potions to repair a damaged relationship
- And much more!

Are you ready to harness the strength of power magick?

These power spells are here to change your life for the better. Whether you want to be more assertive at work or tap into the power of the Spirits, this magick will leave you feeling confident and strong!

Here are some of the power spells you'll find in this complete book of witchcraft:

- Amulets for persuasive power
- Rituals for fame
- Incantations for dominance
- Many more!

Learn the Art of Love Magick and Power Magick Today!

Unlock the secrets of witchcraft within the pages of this Wiccan book of shadows written for those seeking love and power! If you're ready to take control and live your best life, read *Magick for Love and Power* today!

By Didi Clarke

Forbidden Wiccan Spells: Magick for Wealth and Prosperity (Vol. 2)

Find true prosperity with these original money spells from Didi Clarke!

Are you ready to embrace the bounty of the Spirit world? Then this is the book for you! *Forbidden Wiccan Spells: Magick for Wealth and Prosperity* lays out everything you need to know in order to master the art of prosperity magick.

What You'll Find

Within the pages of *FWS: Magick for Wealth and Prosperity*, you'll find never-before-seen money spells that will help put you on the right track for financial success. From herbal magick to incantations, the rituals in this book teach you a wide variety of Wiccan magick—it's perfect for everyone from the complete beginner to the seasoned witch!

These spells include:

- A fire incantation for financial windfall
- An herbal sachet for business success
- Mantras for material prosperity
- Crystal blessings for attracting wealthy people
- And much more!

Are You Ready to Transform Your Life With Money Magick?

These spells won't make you a millionaire overnight—nothing can do that—but that doesn't mean you can't seek help from the Spirit world for money matters! This misunderstood but incredibly effective branch of magick has helped countless witches, Wiccans, and other spiritually minded people take charge of their finances in amazing ways.

Explore These Powerful Spells Today!

Each of these rituals has been written and tested by Didi Clarke herself. They're presented in an easy-to-read, step-by-step format and include a detailed item list and suggestions for achieving maximum potency. What are you waiting for? Embrace the wealth of the Universe today with *FWS: Magick for Wealth and Prosperity*!

Forbidden Wiccan Spells: Dark Goddess Magick (Vol. 3)

Darkness isn't a place of evil—it's a creative force for good that empowers Wiccans and Witches just like you! If you want to learn never-before-seen invocations, spells, and rituals that honor powerful Goddesses, this is the book for you!

Forbidden Wiccan Spells: Dark Goddess Magick explores the many Goddesses associated with darkness—Goddesses of the moon, of sleep, of dreams, and yes, even of death. For too long, those afraid of divine feminine power have told us that these Goddesses are "demons" or "monsters" or practitioners of "black magick." But Didi Clarke is here to set the record straight. These divine beings are powerful allies for any witch that approaches them with a clean heart and pure will.

Within the pages of *FWS: Dark Goddess Magick*, you'll find twelve completely original invocations that have been written and performed by Didi herself. In addition to popular Goddesses like Hecate (Goddess of the dead) and Freyja (Goddess of war), you'll find rituals involving lesser-known dark Goddesses like:
- Breksta (Goddess of dreams)
- Oya (Goddess of storms)
- Selene (Goddess of the moon)
- And many more!

Each chapter provides an easy-to-understand history of a particular Goddess, as well as correspondences associated with her. Next, you'll find an item list and step-by-step instructions for a ritual invoking one of these powerful beings. These rituals touch on many different elements of the Craft and include:
- Protection of your home
- Prophetic dreams
- Developing magickal abilities
- Communing with the dead
- Wiccan candle magick
- Wiccan herb magick
- Wiccan crystal magick
- Much more!

By Didi Clarke

Whether you're looking for a book about Wicca for beginners or are a seasoned witch, whether you're a solitary witch or work with a coven, FWS: Dark Goddess Magick has something for you. It's a great addition to your spell book or your book of shadows! Embrace the power of the dark Goddess within and read it today!

Forbidden Wiccan Spells: Tarot Cards and Psychic Development Rituals (Vol. 4)

Are you ready to master the skills it takes to become a world-class tarot card reader? Are you looking for proven rituals and techniques that will enhance your psychic development?

Forbidden Wiccan Spells: Tarot Cards and Psychic Development Rituals has the answers you're looking for!

Psychic development and the art divination are two of the most misunderstood Spiritual practices out there. But despite the stereotypes, these tools are used every day by rational, ordinary people trying to make better decisions and improve their lives.

In this book, Didi Clarke provides you with everything you need to start transforming your own life with the wisdom of the psychic realm!

What You'll Find

Within the pages of *FWS: Tarot Cards and Psychic Development Rituals*, you'll find a comprehensive breakdown of everything you need to become a confident, insightful tarot card reader. From card meanings to developing your own reading style, this book is perfect for beginners or experienced readers who want a refresher course.

In addition to this tarot handbook, you'll also find completely original spells and rituals meant to enhance your psychic abilities. Whether you want to get better at dream interpretation, reading tea leaves, or anything between, these magickal rituals will help you harness the power of the Spirit world to reach that goal!

Unlock The Future With Tarot Card Readings

Tarot cards are by far one of the most popular forms of divination available. Unfortunately, becoming a proficient reader can seem like an uphill battle—but it doesn't have to be like that!

Within the pages of *FWS: Tarot Cards and Psychic Development Rituals*, Didi Clarke addresses the most important things every tarot card reader needs to know, including:

- Card meanings for all 78 cards
- Major themes of the four minor arcana suits
- Choosing the right card spread
- Memorizing meanings vs. intuitive reading
- Identifying relationships and themes across cards

Hone Your Divination Skills With Psychic Development

Tarot is a fantastic tool, but there is so much more to explore in the world of divination too!

If you're ready to expand your psychic abilities in more ways than one, these spells and rituals should leave you feeling insightful and powerful. The rituals include:

- Invoking Gods of prophecy
- Herbal magick to aid dream interpretation
- Automatic writing
- Meditation for encountering spirit guides
- Candle magick for finding lost objects

Achieve Your Full Spiritual Potential Today!

If you're ready to unlock the secrets of the Spirit world through divination of any kind, the time is now! *FWS: Tarot Cards and Psychic Development Rituals* has all the tools you need to become the master of your own life. Read it today!

Herbs for Witchcraft: The Green

By Didi Clarke

Witches' Grimoire of Plant Magick

Welcome to the world of the green witch—where nature and magick meet!

Plants are a life-giving source of power for every witch. In *Herbs for Witchcraft*, you'll find everything you need to become adept at harnessing this power! The world of plant magick is one of the oldest and most exciting branches of witchcraft—and you too can learn this ancient art!

What You'll Find

This book serves as your guide to all things plant magick. From learning what herbs are best for certain purposes to planning spells based on the season, *Herbs for Witchcraft* takes you through everything you need to get started in the world of green witchcraft. All of these spells and rituals are 100% original and come from Didi Clarke's firsthand experience with the magick of plants.

In particular, you'll discover:

- Plant-based spells and rituals
- Plant folklore
- The beliefs of green witchcraft
- Nature-based Gods and Goddesses
- How to communicate with the natural world
- And much more!

Are you ready to explore the wonder and power of the natural world?

Herbs for Witchcraft is your complete guidebook to the art of plant magick—it's the perfect pick for witches and other spiritual seekers looking to get closer to nature! Buy it today and begin your journey!

Don't forget to sign up for my mailing list and receive your free color magick correspondence chart by following the link below!

https://mailchi.mp/01863952b9ff/didi-clarke-mailing-list

Printed in Great Britain
by Amazon

25828808R00040